About the Life Just Happens Planner and Organizer

Sometimes, life just happens. An accident. Hospitalisation. A stolen purse. Health changes. And sadly, death. These events are stressful enough and can be compounded when we have no idea where to find important information.

This organiser will help you and your loved ones pull together all the information needed in the first few days when life just happens. The organiser is designed for family that live at the same address. It is not designed to replace any emergency planning for worst-case scenarios, but rather aims to provide consolidated information for your loved ones at a difficult time.

GETTING THE MOST OUT OF YOUR ORGANISER:

Provide as much information as possible. Take your time to complete the organiser, as leaving out key details such as account numbers, passwords can make it harder for your family to support you if an emergency arises. Update the planner regularly. Save the interactive electronic version of this file on your computer. Use a pencil to complete information that changes regularly. Keep the organiser in a safe place, with other important documents.

Although this cannot take away the pain and stress you may go through, it is hoped that it does help to provide you with some support when life just happens.

Table of Contents

Section 1: Personal & Passport Information

Personal information about you and your family – full names, contact details, social security or national insurance numbers, email addresses, date and place of birth etc.

Record details for passports – names, passport numbers, nationalities and issue dates. Include a record of any insurance policies you may have.

PERSONAL INFORMATION

	NAME	NAME	NAME
Full Name			
Previous Names			
Familial Relationship			
Address			
Home No.			
Mobile/Cell No.			
Email Address			
Date of Birth			
Place of Birth			
National Insurance.			
Social Security No.			
Driver's Licence No.			
Health Card No.			

PERSONAL INFORMATION

	NAME	NAME	NAME
Full Name			
Previous Names			
Familial Relationship			
Address			
Home No.			
Mobile/Cell No.			
Email Address			
Date of Birth			
Place of Birth			
National Insurance.			
Social Security No.			
Driver's Licence No.			
Health Card No.			

INSURANCE POLICIES

POLICY HOLDER	TYPE OF INSURANCE	NAME OF INSURANCE COMPANY	POLICY NUMBER

PASSPORT INFORMATION

NAME	NATIONALITY	ISSUE DATE	PASSPORT NO.

Section 2: Key Contact Information

Provide information about key contacts such as emergency contacts, a work contact, doctors etc.

Include other key contacts that will need to be contacted.

CONTACTS

EMERGENCY CONTACT		EMERGENCY CONTACT	
Name		Name	
Contact		Contact	
Phone No.		Phone No.	
Email		Email	

DOCTOR		DOCTOR	
Name		Name	
Contact		Contact	
Phone No.		Phone No.	
Email		Email	

DENTIST		DENTIST	
Name		Name	
Contact		Contact	
Phone No.		Phone No.	
Email		Email	

CONTACTS

SCHOOL

Name

Contact

Phone No.

Email

SCHOOL

Name

Contact

Phone No.

Email

WORK CONTACT

Name

Contact

Phone No.

Email

WORK CONTACT

Name

Contact

Phone No.

Email

ACCOUNTANT

Name

Contact

Phone No.

Email

ACCOUNTANT

Name

Contact

Phone No.

Email

CONTACTS

LAWYER

Name

Contact

Phone No.

Email

VET

Name

Contact

Phone No.

Email

PLUMBER

Name

Contact

Phone No.

Email

LAWYER

Name

Contact

Phone No.

Email

ELECTRICIAN

Name

Contact

Phone No.

Email

OTHER

Name

Contact

Phone No.

Email

Section 3: Household Maintenance Schedule

Provide information about what key household activities should be carried out, dates due and the name of the contractor.

MAINTENANCE SCHEDULES

ACTIVITY	DATE DUE	CONTRACTOR	CONTRACTOR NO.
Boiler or Water Heater Service			
Gas Inspection			
Electrical Certification			
Garden			
Heating, Ventilation & AC			
Car Service			
Car Service			
Other			
Other			
Other			

Section 4: Household Bills and Bank Accounts

This section is for banking accounts related to household expenditure and is also to be used to record any financial commitments.

Provide details of monthly commitments such as mortgages, credit cards or loans; utility bills such as gas, electricity or water rates and cable and like commitments.

CURRENT /CHECKING ACCOUNTS

Account Name

Bank Name

Branch Address

Phone No.

Account No.

Online Account

Username

Credit Card No

Routing No./ Sort Code

Password

Pin Number

Account Name

Bank Name

Branch Address

Phone No.

Account No.

Online Account

Username

Credit Card No

Routing No./ Sort Code

Password

Pin Number

CURRENT / CHECKING ACCOUNTS

Account Name

Bank Name

Branch Address

Phone No.

Account No.

Online Account

Username

Credit Card No

Routing No./

Sort Code

Password

Pin Number

Account Name

Bank Name

Branch Address

Phone No.

Account No.

Online Account

Username

Credit Card No

Routing No./

Sort Code

Password

Pin Number

SAVINGS ACCOUNTS

Account Name

Bank Name

Branch Address

Phone No.

Account No.

Online Account

Username

Routing No./
Sort Code

Password

Account Name

Bank Name

Branch Address

Phone No.

Account No.

Online Account

Username

Routing No./
Sort Code

Password

COMMITMENTS – MONTHLY

COMMITMENT	BANK ACCOUNT PAID FROM	PROVIDER PAID TO	AMOUNT	DATE DUE
Mortgage/Rent				
Mortgage/Rent				
Car Loan				
Car Loan				
College Loan				
College Loan				
Personal Loan				
Personal Loan				
Personal Loan				
Personal Loan				
Credit Card				

COMMITMENTS - MONTHLY

COMMITMENT	BANK ACCOUNT	PROVIDER PAID TO	AMOUNT	DATE DUE
Credit Card				
Credit Card				
Credit Card				
Credit Card				
Credit Card				
Other				
Other				
Other				
Other				
Other				
Other				

COMMITMENTS - UTILITIES

COMMITMENT	BANK ACCOUNT PAID FROM	PROVIDER PAID TO	AMOUNT	DATE DUE
Broadband/ Internet Service				
Cable/Satellite				
Council Tax/ Property Tax				
Gas				
Water				
Electricity				
Mobile Phone/ Land Line				
Mobile Phone/ Land Line				
TV Licence				
Landlord's Service Charge				
Streaming Services e.g Netflix				

COMMITMENTS - OTHER

UTILITY	ACCOUNT PAID FROM	PROVIDER	AMOUNT	DATE DUE
Road Breakdown Cover/CAA/AAA				
Road Breakdown Cover/ CAA/AAA				
Road Tax				
Road Tax				
Gym				
Gym				
School Lunches				
School Lunches				
Nanny				
Extra-curricular				
Professional Membership				
Professional Membership				

COMMITMENTS - INSURANCE

COMMITMENTS	ACCOUNT PAID FROM	PROVIDER/ POLICY NUMBER	AMOUNT	DATE DUE
Home/Rental Insurance				
Buildings Insurance				
Life Insurance				
Disability Insurance				
Health Insurance				
Health Insurance				
Car Insurance				
Car Insurance				
Other				
Other				
Other				

Section 5: Assets and Investments

Provide details for your assets – stocks and investments, property, boats vehicles and any other assets you may have including jewellery.

ASSETS - PROPERTY

MORTGAGE – MAIN RESIDENCE

Name(s) on Property Deed

Main Residence Address

Mortgage Amount

Date Due

Lender

Mortgage Reference

Location for Spare Keys

Location of Title Deeds & Mortgage Documents

MORTGAGE – SECONDARY RESIDENCE

Name(s) on Property Deed

Secondary Residence Address

Mortgage Amount

Date Due

Lender

Mortgage Reference

Location for spare keys

Location of Title Deeds & Mortgage Documents

ASSETS - PROPERTY

MORTGAGE – INVESTMENT PROPERTY	
Name(s) on Property Deed	
Investment Property Address	
Mortgage Amount	Date Due
Lender	Mortgage Reference
Location for spare keys	
Location of Title Deeds & Mortgage Documents	
Property Management Agent	
Tenancy Agreement Location	

LAND	
Name on Land Deed	
Land Location	
Mortgage Amount	Date Due
Size	Mortgage Reference
Location of Title Deeds & Mortgage Documents	

ASSETS - VEHICLES

CARS	
Car Owner	
Make	Model
Value of Car	Loan/Lease Company
Car Title Location	Date Due

CARS	
Car Owner	
Make	Model
Value of Car	Loan/Lease Company
Car Title Location	Date Due

CARS	
Owner	
Make	Model
Value of Car	Loan Company
Car Title Location	Date Due

OTHER ASSETS

ITEM	ITEM LOCATION	LOCATION OF TITLES	AMOUNT OWED	VALUE

INVESTMENTS - PAPER DOCUMENTS

INVESTMENT	COMPANY	BROKER	CERTIFICATE NUMBER	VALUE
Pension – Work				
Pension – Private				
Stocks				
Stocks				
Stocks				
Mutual Funds				
Mutual Funds				
ISA/TFSA				
ISA/TFSA				
Alternative Investment e.g. Cryptocurrency				
Alternative Investments e.g. Cryptocurrency				
Other				

INVESTMENTS – ONLINE ACCOUNTS

ACCOUNT	ONLINE ACCOUNTS	USERNAMES	PASSWORDS
Pension – Work			
Pension – Private			
Stocks			
Stocks			
Stocks			
Mutual Funds			
Mutual Funds			
Investment Savings Account			
Investment Savings Account			
Alternative Investments e.g Cryptocurrency			
Alternative Investments e.g Cryptocurrency			
Other			

Section 6: Medical Information

Provide key medical information such as your height and weight, if you are an organ donor, or if you have a DNR order (Do Not Resuscitate).

MEDICAL HISTORY - 1ST PERSON

	DETAILS
Name	
Weight	
Height	
Allergies	
Allergies	
Personal Medical Conditions	
Surgeries	
Surgeries	
Organ Donor	Yes ☐ No ☐
Do Not Resuscitate	Yes ☐ No ☐
Family Medical History	
Medications	
Other	

MEDICAL HISTORY – 2ND PERSON

	DETAILS
Name	
Weight	
Height	
Allergies	
Allergies	
Personal Medical Conditions	
Surgeries	
Surgeries	
Organ Donor	Yes ☐ No ☐
Do Not Resuscitate	Yes ☐ No ☐
Family Medical History	
Medications	
Other	

Section 7: Pet Care

If you have pets, include any specific instructions such as pet insurance details and information about your pet.

PET CARE

	DETAILS
Pet's Name	
Name of Vet	
Contact Number for Vet	
Pet Insurance	
Pet Insurance Policy Number	
Location of Policy Documents	
Pet Name/Type	
Pet Name/Type	
Name of Person(s) that will look after Pet(s)	
Special Instructions for Pet(s) Care	

PET CARE

	DETAILS
Pet's Name	
Name of Vet	
Contact Number for Vet	
Pet Insurance	
Pet Insurance Policy Number	
Location of Policy Documents	
Pet Name/Type	
Pet Name/Type	
Name of Person(s) that will look after Pet(s)	
Special Instructions for Pet(s) Care	

Section 8: Location of Important Documents

Provide details about the location of any important documents your loved ones may need.

IMPORTANT DOCUMENTS

DOCUMENT	REFERENCE NUMBER	LOCATION
Name		
Birth Certificate		
Marriage Certificate		
Citizenship Certificate/ Green Card/Permanent Residency		
Deeds		
Business Documents		
Tax Returns		
Stock and Shares Certificates		
Medical Documents		
Other Legal Documents		
Business Documents		
Other		
Other		

IMPORTANT DOCUMENTS

DOCUMENT	REFERENCE NUMBER	LOCATION
Name		
Birth Certificate		
Marriage Certificate		
Citizenship Certificate/ Green Card/Permanent Residency		
Deeds		
Business Documents		
Tax Returns		
Stock and Shares Certificates		
Medical Documents		
Other Legal Documents		
Business Documents		
Other		
Other		

Section 9: Online Accounts

Technology plays a big part of our lives. Many of the websites we use require personal details or credit card details. Provide details so that these accounts can be closed out to reduce the risk of fraud.

ONLINE ACCOUNTS - TECHNOLOGY AND SOCIAL MEDIA

ACCOUNT	USERNAME	PASSWORD
Computer/Laptop		
Computer/Laptop		
Mobile/Cellular Phone		
Mobile/Cellular Phone		
Email		
Email		
Email		
Instagram		
Facebook		
Twitter		
LinkedIn		
Other		
Other		

OTHER ONLINE ACCOUNTS

ACCOUNT	USERNAME	PASSWORD
Amazon		
eBay		
Online Store		
Online Store		
Online Store		
Steaming Service e.g Netflix		
Music Subscription		
Newspaper Subscription		
Music Subscription		
Podcast Subscription		
Other		
Other		

Section 10: Final Wishes

Many people find it difficult to talk to their loved ones about their funeral wishes due to fear or because they just don't know how to broach the subject. Admittedly, talking to your loved ones about your final wishes is not really a topic of conversation for the dinner table. None of us like to think about dying, let alone talk about it. However, it is important that you somehow let your loved ones know your final wishes.

One way of doing this is by recording your wishes for safekeeping. The following pages are a good way to capture your wishes for your loved ones, so they know about your final wishes without you needing to have the dreaded conversation with them.

ADVANCE DIRECTIVES

ADVANCE DIRECTIVE	DETAILS
Name	
Do I have an Advance Directive?	Yes ☐　　　　No ☐
Location of Advance Directive	
Name(s) of Medical Power of Attorney	
Contact Details for Medical Power of Attorney	

ADVANCE DIRECTIVE	DETAILS
Name	
Do I have an Advance Directive?	Yes ☐　　　　No ☐
Location of Advance Directive	
Name(s) of Medical Power of Attorney	
Contact Details for Medical Power of Attorney	

LIVING TRUSTS

LIVING TRUST	DETAILS	
Name on Living Trust		
Do I have a Living Trust?	Yes ☐	No ☐
Location of Living Trust Documents		
Name of Trustee(s)		
Contact Details for Living Trust Trustee		

LIVING TRUST	DETAILS	
Name on Living Trust		
Do I have a Living Trust?	Yes ☐	No ☐
Location of Living Trust Documents		
Name of Trustee(s)		
Contact Details for Living Trust Trustee		

WILLS

WILLS	FAMILY MEMBER
Name(s) on Will	
Do I/we have a Will?	Yes ☐ No ☐
Location of Will	
Name of Will Executor (1)	
Contact Details for Executor of Will	
Name of Will Executor (2)	
Contact Details for Executor of Will	

WILL	FAMILY MEMBER
Name(s) on Will	
Do I/we have a Will?	Yes ☐ No ☐
Location of Will	
Name of Will Executor (1)	
Contact Details for Executor of Will	
Name of Will Executor (2)	
Contact Details for Executor of Will	

POWER OF ATTORNEYS

POWER OF ATTORNEY	DETAILS
Name	
Do I have a Power of Attorney?	Yes ☐ No ☐
Where is my Power of Attorney Document?	
Type of Power of Attorney	
Name(s) of the Power of Attorney(s)	
Contact Details for the Power of Attorney	

POWER OF ATTORNEY	DETAILS
Name	
Do I have a Power of Attorney?	Yes ☐ No ☐
Where is my Power of Attorney Document?	
Type of Power of Attorney	
Name(s) of the Power of Attorney(s)	
Contact Details for the Power of Attorney	

SOLICITORS OR ATTORNEYS

ATTORNEY	DETAILS	
Name(s)		
Do I have a Solicitor/Attorney?	Yes ☐	No ☐
Name of Solicitor/Attorney		
Solicitor's/Attorney's Contact Details		

ATTORNEY	DETAILS	
Name(s)		
Do I have a Solicitor/Attorney?	Yes ☐	No ☐
Name of Solicitor/Attorney		
Solicitor's/Attorney's Contact Details		

FINAL WISHES – 1ST FAMILY MEMBER

1ST FAMILY MEMBER	WISHES
Name	
Donate my Body/Organs	☐ Donate my Body ☐ Donate my Organs
Funeral to be Paid for by:	☐ Funeral Plan ☐ Life Insurance ☐ Other Savings ☐ Estate ☐ Friends & Family
Location of Funeral Plan or Insurance	
I want a Funeral Director to arrange the funeral	☐ Yes ☐ No
Name of Funeral Home	
Contact Number for Funeral Home	
Type of Funeral	☐ Traditional ☐ Cremation – specify wishes for ashes ☐ Woodland ☐ Burial at Sea ☐ Entombment

FINAL WISHES – 1ST FAMILY MEMBER

	WISHES
Name	
Burial Arrangements	☐ New Grave ☐ With Family Member in Existing Plot/ Crypt
Funeral Location	
Specify Casket Type	
Specify Type of Grave Marker and Inscription	
Funeral Transport	☐ Traditional Hearse and Limousine ☐ Horse-drawn Hearse ☐ Motorcycle Hearse ☐ Other - Specify ______________
Who would you like to Conduct the Funeral Service?	

FINAL WISHES – 1ST FAMILY MEMBER

1ST FAMILY MEMBER	DETAILS
Who would you like as Pallbearers?	
Who would you like as Pallbearers?	
Who would you like as Pallbearers?	
Are there any specific poems or scriptures you would like read?	
Are there any specific songs you would like sung or played?	
What type of flowers would you like?	
Where should any memorial contributions be sent?	
What type of wake would you like?	
Comment	

FINAL WISHES – 1ST FAMILY MEMBER

OTHER NOTES

FINAL WISHES – 2ND FAMILY MEMBER

2ND FAMILY MEMBER	WISHES
Name	
Donate my Body/Organs	☐ Donate my Body ☐ Donate my Organs
Funeral to be Paid for by:	☐ Funeral Plan ☐ Life Insurance ☐ Other Savings ☐ Estate ☐ Friends & Family
Location of Funeral Plan or Insurance	
I want a Funeral Director to arrange the funeral	☐ Yes ☐ No
Name of Funeral Home	
Contact Number for Funeral Home	
Type of Funeral	☐ Traditional ☐ Cremation – specify wishes for ashes ☐ Woodland ☐ Burial at Sea ☐ Entombment

FINAL WISHES – 2ND FAMILY MEMBER

2ND FAMILY MEMBER	WISHES
Name	
Burial Arrangements	☐ New Grave ☐ With Family Member in Existing Plot/ Crypt
Funeral Location	
Specify Casket Type	
Specify Type of Grave Marker and Inscription	
Funeral Transport	☐ Traditional Hearse and Limousine ☐ Horse-drawn Hearse ☐ Motorcycle Hearse ☐ Other - Specify _______________
Who would you like to Conduct the Funeral Service?	

FINAL WISHES – 2ND FAMILY MEMBER

2ND FAMILY MEMBER	DETAILS
Name	
Who would you like as Pallbearers?	
Who would you like as Pallbearers?	
Who would you like as Pallbearers?	
Are there any specific poems, or scriptures you would like read?	
Are there any specific songs you would like sung or played?	
What type of flowers would you like?	
Where should any memorial contributions be sent?	
What type of wake would you like?	

FINAL WISHES – 2ND FAMILY MEMBER

OTHER NOTES

Section 11: Additional Information

You may need to leave home immediately in the event of an emergency. Be prepared to leave home by having a smaller version of your emergency kit in an easy-to-access place. It may also be useful to create grab-and-go-bags for your workplace and vehicles.

It's also wise to plan for emergencies that could keep you at home. Always keep some food and water, as well as other items such as candles and matches, and numbers for your local emergency services.

IDEAS FOR AT HOME EMERGENCIES

AT HOME EMERGENCY IDEAS

Dried food such as rice or pasta

Canned food such as canned meats, beans or soups

Drinking water

Phone charger and battery bank

Small battery-powered or hand-crank radio

Battery-powered or hand-crank flashlight

Extra batteries

Small first-aid kit and personal medications

Candles and matches

Copy of your 'Just in case of an emergency Planner and Organiser' with copies of important documents, such as insurance papers
Small first-aid kit and personal medications

Some cash in small bills

IDEAS FOR A GRAB-AND-GO BAG

GRAB-AND-GO BAG IDEAS

Food (ready to eat) and water

Phone charger and battery bank

Small battery-powered or hand-crank radio

Battery-powered or hand-crank flashlight

Extra batteries

Small first-aid kit and personal medications

Personal toiletries and items, such a pair of glasses or contact lenses

Copy of your 'Just in case of an emergency Planner and Organiser' with copies of important documents, such as insurance papers
Small first-aid kit and personal medications

Some cash in small bills

local map with your family meeting place highlighted

Seasonal clothing and an emergency blanket

A pen and notepad

A whistle

NOTES

www.ingramcontent.com/pod-product-compliance
Lightning Source LLC
Chambersburg PA
CBHW040135240726
48664CB00002B/496